BENT BOX

Lee Maracle

THEYTUS BOOKS
PENTICTON

Canadian Cataloguing in Publication Data

Maracle, Lee, 1950–
  Bent box

  Poems.
  ISBN 0-919441-89-0

  I. Title.
PS8576.A6175B46 2000 C811'.54   C00-910367-8
PR9199.3.M3497B46 2000

Editorial: Greg Young-Ing
Design: Val Speidel
Special Thanks: Chick Gabriel, Florene Belmore, Lally Grauer

Theytus Books Ltd.
Lot 45 Green Mountain Rd.
RR#2, Site 50, Comp. 8
Penticton, BC
V2A 6J7

The publisher acknowledges the support of The Canada Council for the Arts, The Department of Canadian Heritage and the BC Arts Council in the publication of this book.

Contents

Turbulent Storm

Bent Box

Warm Wind

DEEP REGRET

Performing

I shudda got 'n Oscar
for all the lies I told,
all the masks I wore . . .
But they don't give
Indian women Oscars
for dressin' like Vogue Magazine
and drippin'
honeyed English.

        Remember T'a-ah
        I speak brocken
        Ink-lish tooh?

Now

        I am

                speechless . . .

Sister

I die a little to think we could never be
two sisters in love with life
sharing the same dream
one clean, sweet vision of freedom

I die a little to think we let them
divide us, that we had not the love
to bind us

So helpless were we as small babies
no power,
no strength to oppose the forces
keeping us apart

Naive and innocent the world fell upon us
ripped us from the same womb tearing asunder
the sacred bond of family

It did not come easy, with pain and torment
we faced a common enemy, disunited and spiteful
before sweet womanhood came upon us
we gave up

I would like to hold my sister
feel her warm embrace and touch her spirit
just one time

Rage

I scream my rage
at the pages of a book
that I might treat
people—humanly.

Words

On my desk sits a big, fat dictionary
　　　　thick—oh, it's thick
　　　　obese with words.

Opening and closing it is the sum total
of my physical movement these days.

　　　　I'm tired
　　　　tired
　　　　torn
　　　　weary
　　　　without initiative

The phone rings I bubble out a stupid hello.

　　　　"How are you?"

　　　　"Oh, I'm fine," but it is a lie.

　　　　The hunger in my life
　　　　The absence of joy.

　　　　The fire in me blanketed by billboards,
　　　　of blonde women and pink, perfumed rose petals

But no one wants to hear that—they want only words

　　　　(pretty, sweet lyrics)
　　　　(senseless limericks)
　　　　(and honeyed poetics)

Paralysis

(CHAPTER I)

T'a-ah used to say
"You am or you amn't"

Now I am drunk
Words dribble from loose lips
grating against flesh
imprisoned by self-imposed
physical paralysis

Words: replace my bodily need to
MOVE!

(CHAPTER II)

Idle Men enchained
by Uncle Willie
                  blinded
by the darkness
of immobility
                  enslaved
to white
                  parasite
          culture
                  gripped
by the agony
        of colonial
                  paralysis

Untitled

let's not discuss a single thing
let us not be rational
that presumes we're human,
                              warm,
                    sensitive beings,
in need of patience,
                    gentleness,
                              and love.

The object is not unity
but win this fight.
Retaliate. Kick your lover's pride,
dismantle his dignity
and drink,
          drink,
                    drink . . .
to the ghosts
          in your closet.

Autumn Rose

(This poem was inspired by a child named Autumn Rose. The poem is not about her but rather my perception of our self-destruction and the children who are the natural resistance to destruction. Our children are the basis for my optimism.)

If the state won't kill us,
then, we will have to kill ourselves.

It's no longer good etiquette
to head hunt savages,
so we'll just have to do it ourselves.

It's not polite to violate squaws,
so we'll just have to find an Indian to oblige us.

It's poor form to let an Indian starve,
we'll have to deprive our young ourselves.

Blinded by niceties and polite liberality
we can't see our enemy,
so we'll just have to kill each other.

> In this field
> of dying leaves
> dead grass
> and rustling winds
> blooms
> a lone
>   autumn rose.

Since Uncle Willie started giving us hush money
we have stepped up the campaign against ourselves
with a fierceness we haven't known since our
forefather's resistance. I would be cynical but
for the tenacity of the late Autumn Rose who
stubbornly clings to life in a season when all
flora are laid to rest.

The children I meet are the roses in autumn.
A child is forever blossoming. Their parents
may feel crushed but the children go on blooming
like the lovely, stubborn rose.

Untitled

in this room
warm pictures die

Review

(A review of Samir Amin's
theoretical analysis of
imperialism: "Centre and
Periphery")

I would not like
to live in a house
built by Samir Amin
who thinks
the foundation
is on the periphery.

Actress (Nilak Butler)

I am an actress
    a good one.

I have smiled
a thousand times
at people I have never met.

I am an image
I have held my head up
under circumstances
t'would shame a rose.

I can dramatize for you
the suffering of the multitudes
while my own dreams go unnoticed.

I can act out for you
the pain of imprisonment
while my own pain
stays locked up.

Don't think me insensitive
I hear the whisperings,
"psst . . . she was an actor . . .
you know."

Fish-Wife

I am unclean,
daughter of an unwashed fisher woman
                    loud, lean and raw.
I have no manners,
                no finesse.
Iron will and loyalty are all
                    I possess.

I am not a docile forest creature
a quaint curio

I am a burning flame
                not yet *uhuru*
                not yet woman
but very much alive!

Alone

I am alone, so alone.
I want to stay that way.

I love fleeting
glimpsing shadows
                of men.

In the absence
of real love
fraud will do.

Striving

I drank heartily of the settler's wine
learned his language well,
gazed with awe at his success.

I staggered through paragraphs
of his culture brewed in western schools.

My striving went to naught.
It is the trying
that shames me now.

Karen

Two bright lights
a scream in the night
a shattered chest
closed the door
to Karen's life.

She couldn't breathe
it's as simple as that.

It was sunny all over my life
the day I let Stormy down.

No. I let myself down
I heard her calling
in desperation—relieve me,
relieve me of the twisting
pain of powerless tormented life.

Relieve me of the pain!

I didn't have the modesty to say;

I CAN'T!

Dandelion

There's a dandelion on the roadside in Toronto.
Its leaves a dishevelled mix of green and brown.
      A dandelion scraggling 'n limping along.

There's a flower beside a concrete stump
on Bay Street, in Toronto. Perpetually rebellin'
      against spiked heels and blue serge suits.

The monetary march past 5 o'clock Bay Street
(deaf to the cries of this thin aging lion)
      sneers: "Chicken-yellow flower . . ."

My leaves, my face . . . my skin . . . I feel like
my skin is being scraped off of me. There is
      a flower in Toronto. On the roadside.

It takes jack hammers and brutish machines to rip
the concrete from the sidewalks in Toronto
      to beautify the city of blue serge suits.

But, for this dandy lion, it takes but a seed,
a little acid rain, a whole lot of fight and a
black desire to limp along and scraggle

      forward. There is a flower.

On Being Broke

Only respectable citizenry
find the streets abhorrent.

The practicalities of motherhood
drove me off the street,
into the gentle lap of respectability.

Tho'
It's hard to get excited

There exists amid
the death and destruction of the street,
          a moral code—

an odd brand of camaraderie

that does not exist, say . . .
in a west end apartment block.

A Wilted Flower

Behind a balcony
perched high above
a littered street

a cracked
dirty window pane
obscures a woman.

On skid row streets
where no flowers grow
she longs to be a rose.

It is taking
so long for her
to realize:

a flower thrives
most willingly
when fed manure,

and wilt—
be the only fate
of a plucked rose.

Carry Her Away

Cirrhosis
of the liver.

Poisoned,
bloated,
spiritless.

Alone, no weapons to fight
she despaired, drank and died.

(It took only 35 years)

To mangle our hearts
with the vision of her pain.

Sweet grass and sage,
smoke of the aged,

carry her away.

TURBULENT STORM

From a Tainted Rose

Painted my face belies my pain
fluffed up by silks and fine wools
my body can move in elegant half-circles

spiralling about a home bedecked
in soft clean lines
each room bathed in the low of unnatural light

the spirals entangle, twist themselves in knots
these knots stick in my craw
tightening my view, blocking my eyes

will your resistence open my eyes
to blossoming flowers
relieve me of the twisted knots?

You would seek pain to bring peace,
climb mountains to endow character
draw cold before comfort
your resistance carefully nurtured by dead
grannies hopeless dreams
blinds you to the beauty asleep within

Where were your grannies' ideals
when they skinned our mountaintops
which grandmother cast doleful eyes
upon my bleeding self as I witnessed
cedar heaped upon a funeral pyre
to perish naked and alone?

I wept torrentious rivers 'til my eyes dried.
First they came for us, incarcerated
in residential schools, foster homes, jails . . .
When they ripped the trees from the earth
with impunity, the caretakers were weeping
from prisons your resistance could not dismantle.

Dismantle.

I love not these people anymore than you.
I am nonetheless blind for cherishing comfort.

Streets

I know these streets.
Buried beneath them are old pathways,
safe trails which brought my grandmothers from birth to elderhood,
carried them from ancestral village to gardens.

I know these streets.
Each one brought newcomers, new practices,
unfathomable customs which transformed our lives,
erased the gentle trails of Anishnawbekwe.

I remember my *A'holt* dodging humans
as she hurried from one village to the next under cover of dark.
The two men who accosted her, whiskey breath punch drunk
and uninterested in her consent, tearing at her.

I remember their knife as they slit her skirt, she
clutching it, fingers bleeding, exacting justice
their bodies left to perish in the night as she raced home
along the last safe trail.

I remember my momma and her tale, dodging cars
under cover of dark, hiding, hurrying, rushing,
trying to make it home before the invasion of her
private self would forever mar.

I remember these streets, my youthful vigour,
myself in the most beautiful time in my life, jumping
into a ditch, rotted water insulting my sense of being, hiding
as I waited for the engine of the assaulting vehicle to drift into the
            night-silent.

Silent. Under the loud textured voices of the newcomers, we grew
                oddly silent,
while strange that Cheryl Joe's intestines were thrown into these
streets. Rosemarie Roper is broken from her gravel pit
death bed. The end of her walk through the night on these new
                streets,
brought no thundering outrage.

In the dark, on the street, the quiet spells ominous foreboding.
Silence does not protect. Voiceless we quake under the heel
of assault. Voiceless we quiver under the umbrellas of threat.
The night becomes an insult, not a moment for reflection.

We inherited this night a long time ago. A promise from
Grandmother Moon came with it. The promise of dreams,
sweet and wonderful. The promise of love, sure and enduring.
This night, this night, is so bound to these streets, to silence, to
                violence.

So enslaved is this night when death quiet kills dreams
destroys the sweetness, the wonderment, the promise of human love.
Grandmother Moon: you sit above these streets forced to witness the
night that has visited itself upon these new streets.

I apologize for not coming sooner, to free your eyes,
to re-craft the images below,
to raise my voice in resistance
to the desecration of your eternity.

Song to a Palestinian Child

I hear a voice calling from a place far away
The voice of a girl child very much like my own

of green grass and rich soil is Palestine.

Bombs crash about her levelling her home
Clutching an olive branch she raises a defiant fist

of deep roots and copper sun is Palestine.

I see a child rising from a place far away
In one hand an olive branch in the other a gun

of much sweat and red blood is Palestine.

I hear you calling me. Raise my banner high
(Victory), victory to Palestine I answer in kind

of humble tears my salute to Palestine.

Women

Palestinian women rock baby cradles
to the rhythm of US/Israeli bombs
while desert winds tear at tipis
and sand blasts the faces of water-bearers.

> In Can-America; mothers use ivory
> and the rising price of "HUGGIES"
> is our most serious problem.

Amid peppered streets
and flattened villages,
waves of resistance
lash at the citadels of capital.

> The streets of Can-America
> are flooded only with shoppers
> scurrying to buy . . . buy . . . buy . . .

In underground workshops
built by humble hands
women work through the night
to create weapons for Palestine.

> The feminine hands of Can-America
> greedily eat Israeli oranges
> Palestinian children have never seen.

Warm, the earth bearing woman's
soft, sure step dignity
printed in the oasis of struggle
watered by womanly resistance.

And the warm winds of change
breathe the pure scent of victory
to the shores of my decadent home.

Bring the Boys Home

(Nicaragua—Another Vietnam)

Last spring I climbed Shannon Falls,
the mountain of my ancestors.

Beset with vertigo and jelly legs
victory seems impossible.

Success is best appreciated
when it is the least probable.

1986 is a decisive year.
Senor Americo has no way out.
Invasion is the last door.

Canada has no choice
Riding piggy back on Senor Americo
whining like a younger brother
Canada must join hands.

The family must close ranks
under a fanatical patriarch.
Close ranks or surrender.

We have climbed this mountain before.
We have climbed amid
torrentious rains, blinding winds,
with naught but our water
        soaked shirts and lonely gun.
While rain drummed its dreaded orchestra
and the wind sang its song of destruction

we climbed.
Amid the chaos and the cold,
unafraid, we reached the summit.

When the banks of the river are over-run by flood waters
one does not quiver and quake on the valley floor.

The cherished tender feet of *los gringos*
are unwilling to forge flood waters,
climb mountain with naught
but a shirt and a lonely gun.

The mercenaries of Senor Reagan will not
quiver in the cold, nor hunger in the darkness
for the sake of corporate America.

Los minos de Senor Americo *perfiremos el dinero*
guanudo sin pena: no gustamos trabajos
Easy come easy go; that is the slogan
that the children of America prefer.

El Salvador—*Vencera*

"Our struggle, like a tree,
grows from roots nourished
by the rich earth of El Salvador
—our beloved homeland.

One root *es Indigenas*
—the experience of our ancestors.
The other: *El Revolution*
—the lessons of our struggle."

Senor America! You are blind!
You do not see our ancestors,
our grandmother's copper-gold faces
and waist-length black hair.

You do not see our grandfathers
dancing to their ancient flutes
or greeting the cold autumn dawn
to harvest corn: the seed of life.

Senor America! You are deaf.
You do not hear the cries
of the working sons of Spain
impoverished and over-worked by you.

If you were not blind, *Senor*
you could see that in El Salvador
the dual roots of our history
has become a single tree of unity.

You do not see our *Mujeras* . . .
the trunk of our sacred tree
The mothers and wives
of those who died in '32.

These brave-hearted women
who wept; dried their eyes,
then sang sweet songs of lament
that spoke of our fighter's courage.

Senor America! You are bloated!
Waxed fat by our humble defeat.
Stupefied by your success.
Doomed by your arrogance.

It is we who hear the voices
—of our ancestors
educating us to our mistakes
—ensuring your demise.

From the heartbeat of ancient drums
and the musings of Spanish guitars
comes one song—one song . . .
REVOLUTION UNTIL VICTORY!

Los Obreros y los campesinos,
mujeras, Indigenas, y los pobres
hijos de los conquistadores
have all joined hands, *Senor* . . .

And we will hammer at the chains of imperialism
Until YOU
have learned your lesson well:

PATRIA O MUERTE! VENCEREMOS!

Outside the Circle of Chilean Fires

We sit outside the circle of Chilean fires
surrounded by baubles 'n trinkets
the hallmarks of Chilean street death.

No one here is shot for protesting.

We can not see past the golden arches
deafened are we by electronic chords of lost love,
adultery roars at us from Sony Walkmans
drowning the death sounds of Chilean youth.

Beyond the golden arch a bullet splits the sky
a twisted body writhes on the blood-red street.
From purple-blue mountains, from the schools
and factories comes a mother's mournful song:

> If there is death on the streets of Chile
> then there is hope in the hearts of Chileans.
> If there is murder against innocent youth
> it is because there is power among people.

If the military regime is shooting people
then it fears its own days numbered
Salud, salud! La Resistencia

Venceremos!

Saga of American Truth

They stole upon the village huts
under cover of a moonless night
with musket and sword they drowned
the sleepy resistance in blood.

Stripped of their gold
manacled, they marched into the heart
of Africa through stanchions of green
to vessels bobbing innocently, awash
with the red glow of a rising star.

Layer upon layer they stacked Africa's finest
in filthy holds. Feverish. Wounded
the robust daughters of Africa
were readied for death's claim.

Under a demonic dome of bourbon lust
the tumescent erection of youthful madness
birthed—America—Manifest Destiny—
to be nursed by the beast of Africa.

Grandmothers, red earth coloured
bore witness. Spirits quivering,
our naked grandmothers cried
above the howl of spilt black blood.

The fire of our outrage burned
America's face. Cotton dawn and
tired earth dogged his erection.
Resistance rattled the cage of slavery.

Inflamed by America's crotchety lie,
we secreted black mother between tipis
pathed by blessed song, the tears of split
family a cross requiem for black young.

Village to village, sheltered by starless skies
fleeing black youth ran 'longside cayuse
and red earth warriors. But few survived.
Few survived the broken trail to liberty.

America. His brat youth spent
cloaked his madness in rigid maturity.
In a dying dockyard a slave ship revived
to carry our multitudes to the jewel of carib.

By dint of the lash and musket
Black mother's daughters built roads
atop our ancestral lands, fresh
with red earth woman's blood, forced
cotton from earth's barren chest.

Under a de-bizoned, treeless October sky
we watched the parched and looted land.
America's autumn birth a thorny rose.
A sojourner whose truth bid us rise again.

We rose again, were beaten by the pining
of America's delicate orchid.
—the hallmark of America's tumescence
drowned the song of Sojourner.

Sojourner whose truth we could not bury
burned holes in our wintery refuge.

Dogged by her resistance she filled
our bodies with this persistent need.

The ghost of black mother walks the wind
atop red earth woman's ageless cayuse.
They come to us now and then
jogging us from our earthly sleep.

This sojourner whose truth I dare not see.
This ghost of black mother and her homeless,
red earth companion, singing their sacred song:
AIN'T I A WOMAN! *AIN'T I A* WOMAN!

We are here yet, the rising wretched of America.
A pair of stubborn roses, thorny and wrathful,
left over from an America whose withered manhood
has been twisted into a saga of perverse humour.

Like an old sick joke American tries to rise
his worn loins, swollen with misuse
runs amok to invoke the rage of womanhood.
His demise is but a squirt away . . .

(EPILOGUE)

We sit staring out the window
at this dirty old man who cannot stop
raping the world. We watch while he spills
the blood of children in Soweto . . .

The blood fills my bedroom with truth.
It is the blood of Annie Mae, my sister,

my children, running red in my homeland,
securing Indigenous invisibility.

"Inequity" is but a blasphemous
cloak for Canadian apartheid.
A liberal term no one but us
need take seriously. Rise Soweto.

I swim upstream against rivers of blood
Gnashing hopelessly at death with words.
Penned between gasps and desperate strokes
aimed at the same perverse enemy.

Rise Soweto. From my window I see death
for this America who cannot drown us all.
Rise Soweto! My turn is coming, 'tis
just round the corner . . . victory.

Mister Mandela

Forgive me Mister Mandela
I tried to picture you in prison
for twenty-five years
but a hand closed on my throat

I know this hand
It lives in the windowless room
of my childhood
A room filled with rats and menacing sounds

A terrifying loneliness
seizes my insides
closes my voice
and I don't want to remember

In the dark, eyes shut tight
the memories of an empty belly
force themselves to fill the space
where thoughts of you ought to live

The sight of your Black face
between stark white walls and iron bars
draws the drapes on the ray of light
left me by a thousand rain-soaked days

When I look at you in prison, Mr. Mandela
I can't feel the power of mother sea
feel the wind of my green mountains
or rise up to resist their demise

I treasure this eagle of resistance
couching you and Leonard in each wing
You shall have to be happy, Mr. Mandela
with my humble tribute

Leonard

Where else does one hear
the clang of metal on metal

Where else do days stretch
into endless days

Where time is marked
by an insistent nothingness

Where from morning until night
there is no comfort, only cruel laughter
at the torment
of your comrades
who, like you
are incarcerated
caught in a time warp

"Momma my life stopped 11 and $^1/_2$ years ago,"
Brother Malcom said "everyone who is not free
is in jail"

It isn't so
Jail
is an empty room
without light
or love

It is life
without living
suffering without struggle

For those of you who are not free
but may move without steel
there is at least the joy
of rebelling

War

In my body flows the blood of Gallic
Bastille stormers and the soft, gentle
ways of Salish/Cree womanhood.

Deep throated base tones dissipate,
swallowed by the earth; uproarious
laughter sears, mutilates my voice.

Child of the earth-tear of west
coast rain; dew drop sparkling in
the crisp, clear sun of my home.

Warm woman of the Mediterranean sunscape,
bleaching rough cotton-sweatshop
anniversary.

Thunderous, rude earthquakes that
split my spirit within. Tiny grapes
of wine console me.

Can I deny a heritage blackened by
the toil of billions, conceived in
rape, plunder and butchery?

In the veins, that fight to root themselves
in the wondrous breadth of my
homeland, races the blood of base
humanity.

European thief; liar, bloodsucker.
I deny you not. I fear you not. Your
reality and mine no longer rankles me.

I am moved by my love for human life;
by the firm conviction that all the world
must stop the butchery, stop the slaughter.

I am moved by my scars, by my own filth
to re-write history with my body
to shed the blood of those who betray themselves.

To life, world humanity I ascribe
To my people . . . my history . . . I address
my vision.

Victory

No hurt burns my spirit
No pain thirsts my eyes
No lies poison my mind

Where Were You

Where were you when you crossed the line
Were you ferreting your way through the grass
too tangled and too tall for you to see past the
moment into the clear light of your own path

Where were you when the line blurred
Had you retreated to the cold heart-vacuumed
out space, someone named home, crying
in the night, praying someone would lift this weight

This weight, this weight which was not real
could not be real, so heavy, so terrifyingly
wrong, this weight which pulsed breath thick
with old wind and lascivious impropriety

In the midst of this impropriety did you open your throat
or did the fear of this bulk-beast weight tearing
at parts of you, not intended for this use, close your
voice to the possibility of rescue from someone

Someone, someone who should have heard you felt
terrible tension whispering its way out of your small room
Someone should have sensed the locked-throat
little boy writhing under the weight praying

Praying that tumescence would come soon, praying
there was no blood, though down there felt so torn
So wide open, so pained that surely "I must be dead,
I must be gone, this can not be happening"

This cannot be happening to me, me must not be
happening to it. It, this bulk-beast weight, is
unrecognizable, unseen in the windowless room
It must be a bogeyman, not my uncle drunk again

Where were you when the line slipped from your grasp and law
failed your adult imagined principled self, your image
so carefully constructed of layers of public acceptability,
cracked and the wounded child spilled out

Spilled out onto this other wounded child you had brought
to weep, to wish, to want some comfort from a man
A man her father's age, to receive, to receive a recycled
version of the father who had no right to make her his small wife

Where were you when the line lay wounded
Were you stuck in the loneliness of an open field
tied up, aunts crawling about your small thin body
torturing you while you wept inside, prayed for relief

Relief from this black space, this emotion empty house
This torment, the dodging of relatives who were supposed
to bring peace, joy and only used you as a plaything
for the game of pass it on, these pain generals assaulted

Assaulted your crippled spirit, blotted out
the possibility of you ever being able to envision
yourself, your self, which lays open and dichotomized
Unreal, unreliable, trapped and unloved

Where were you when the line grew sick
Were you in the gullies of your grassy homeland
hunting nests of snakes, filling them with lighter
fluid, lighting a match and squealing with delight

Squealing delight into entrances to old tunnels
dark and foreboding, listening to strange muffled
language, while your body responded sensuously
opened up to the seduction of your own fear

Did the fear filled gasoline bottles shoot waves of adrenal
mad-strength-lust into your veins, skim across your skin
cutting alluring images of possibility, of blowing up
those muffled sounds, bombing those dark tunnels

Bombing those tunnels into forever quiet, quiet
moments ensconced in your imaginary world of unreality
un-familied, you wrenched family from between
the dark moments, the cold and the odd sex in between

The cold and the odd sex in between the dark moments
of huge nothingness while daily you dodge the bulk-beast
tormenters who passed you from one beast to another
weighted you until reality no longer existed for you

Where were you when you crossed the line, were you
floating in the thin line between lost family dreams
Dreams you dared not make real or you would
come to recognize the bulk-beast weight upon you

In your recognition you would see your self, your
lostness, your losses piling one on top of the other
your regrets chained end to end, the absence of you
linked to each loss, your face erased by the avoidance of loss

This face, this face who was never permitted to see
himself running, jumping, playing or enjoying life
its awesome mystery shadowed by your own
mystical unreality, calling you to conjure images

Images for each other in your life, images which
you disciplined yourself to adhere to until all the pictures
folded one into the other and all the others in your life
imploded and the glue holding them together disappeared

Disappeared into the wellspring of confusion
just under image where the crack leaks truth
anger pushes it all back in, solders the crack until
you can retreat and re-conjure a whole new image

I image you alone, in a dark place counting your losses
pretending they are wins, perverting the imagery of all
those who ever loved you, seducing yourself with
the voice saying, "nobody cares about me"

Nobody hears the sweet sounding I have no ones you
repeat to yourself while some other voice justifies
ameliorates and trivializes the choice you made to cross
the line instead of finding your authentic self

Your authentic spirit would not have brought you
to violate the vagina of a child making light of
things you transformed into ugliness
this ugly is attached to a cruel misunderstanding of love

The ugly story is named and rejected by us
We name its stern cruelty, its lust breath violation
its moment violence, its weight thick and heavy
is the creation of a terrifying numbness

Numb you stand under an umbrella you
never had a hand in constructing
Do you imagine it gives you freedom, the freedom to be
numb, the freedom to never enjoy sunsets or rain

To never return to the dark of your room, to weep
to reclaim the living, feeling self you left behind
denying his emotions, but never will this little boy
give up on his self, give up his desire to be

Tumbleweed

Fat tugs chug
up and down the inlet; huffing
puffing, lugging the trees.

Massive freighters
drag precious booty
—earth's treasure
to the four corners of the globe.

Shattered clouds
pour out poisoned tears of once
clean, sweet, west coast rain.

Vang-coover.
Khatsalano's birth place.
Whiteman's nightmare, city
                              of my birth.

Death

Death hangs over us
like a black, widow-maker
on a treeless mountainside.

A beleaguered army
caught in a valley
we thought green, lush
and teeming with life
          suddenly becomes a swamp
          full of alligators
          leeches, filth, disease.

Disease and death. DIS-EASE.

Caused more by the shame
of being fooled one more time.

In the darkness of our own
confusion we have forgotten
          our reason for being.

Ancestors

Bent, bleeding bodies burnt brown by the sun in sugar beet fields,
tear toxic sweet from earth's bosom for childly consumption.

Cracked cold hands cut swimmer, spilling guts and snapping heads
from ocean's bounty to rot on concrete cannery decks.

From my brother's chain-saw comes a screaming massacre for
            lordly cedar,
to perish in the interest of profit.

Lest I learn, enemy of mine, pay me with alcohol, drug me,
lest I hear the ancient call of my ancestors—to arms?

The Language Leaked from my Lips

The language leaked from my lips in letters too short and too young to help me understand that remembering had some significance.

The language you gave me failed me, failed to assist me in those moments when invasion fell upon my private self.

Now my language, so richly textured with instruction, is stripped of emotion's unraveling expression of possibility.

This possibility's poesy, story, hopeful imagination, died in the dark on the floor in the puddle of my leaked letters.

My lips emptied of light cannot imagine dark whose actuality was my pathway to future dreamworld carving.

My forever light precludes dreaming in the dark, the starkness of constant light burns holes through the curtain of hope outside my word puddle.

Letters dance lonely in the stark light at the edge of this pool. Their death throes mourn my dead dark night.

I crawl about collecting letters, rearranging them, playing with meaning, grabbing whatever I can from wherever they appear.

These letters feel foreign, scrape at the meaning in my mind, tear at the yearning of my soul and dance just out of reach of my heart.

BENT BOX

Bent Box

you
can't
put
waterfalls
in a
bent box
empty deserts
and bald mountains
won't fit.

you
can't
put
sister sun
in a
bent box
images of
rain can't be seen
from
its
earth-dark
contours.

Bent Box (Thought)

Thought travels in circles
of curious light.
Butterflying its way
across
infinite horizons
through finite
channels
directed by purpose.

Thought does not need deadwood
leaves to darken
perfect blankness
it meanders through infinite
memory, doggedly finds
finite expression
in a bent box.

Words peeled from a poet's
pen shape the bends
of
my
box.

Bent Box (Choice)

Choice
marches boldly
ahead of meaningless
drivel
sneaks
through the cracks
of
all
boxes
including
bent ones.

Bent Box (Legions)

Laughter
slips
through the grain
pattern
of bent box
eternity.
Legions
of ancestors
chee-chee-cheeing about you
pardon
poppycock and tommyrot
because
you can't help
being
"that way."

Bent Box (Dear Racist)

I cherish my bent box image of your infant self before you were
uprooted, cast adrift, mangled by the limbo your ancestors
bequeathed you.

Your timeless memory lives inside, shrieking endless pleas;
to be relieved of the prison you consign it to.

Bent Box (Racist I)

Hostility
rages inside his cell
the terror of confusion
ambiguity
and nonsense
hide his secret self
retreats
to bent box musing
until his rage is spent.

He sits
next me,
starving
inside
his obese house.
This once sacred
dwelling consumed
his bent spirit,
emptied it of hope
filled
it
with rage.

"I want to be a racist,"
a heart-rending sob
layered by anger
and memories
too dangerous
for him to contemplate
becomes a bellow.
Illness
dismantled
the sacred home
of his spirit.
An illness
too complex
and terminal
for the magic of my bent box.

I hear
his sobs atop
his vengeful
inhuman
words
the truth of me swallowed
by my bent box
image of his infancy
staring,
pleading.
"I want to go home."

"I want to go home
inside myself
wander about on sacred trails
of
infinite
primal knowledge.
I want to go home
to that perfect place
before
the slashing
hammering
of healing stones
concealed me."

He looks from eyes
unable to peer out
from the spiralling
infant truth
of layer upon layer
of familiar
ancient knowledge,
but sees
from some limbo
rooted know-where,
know-where.

I don't
like looking
at him,
each time I do,
my bent box
wraps itself
around me.
I imagine
infant purity
before abuse adulterated
his soul.

I try not to listen
to the sweet gentle cries
of new birth
pleading for whole life,
but my box
vibrates,
amplifying
his cries.

Letters fall out of his mouth
pathetically typed
separate
flat
neat little individuals
scatter themselves
on the floor
before
they reach me
unheard
over the sound of his crying.

Grey skin,
once rose-hued
a stretched patchwork quilt
over a too
vast expanse
of flesh
betrays him,
hunger dogs his body,
screams at his soul,
despite
his bulk.

Feet planted
firmly in mid-air
he cannot stand to look
to see
we did not rob him
of his self
we did not
sever
his roots.
We don't own
this hatred
this wrathful
acid
rage
is contained in a vessel
of his own
construction.

I cherish
my bent box image
of your infant self
before
you were uprooted
cast adrift
mangled
by the limbo
your ancestors
bequeathed
you.

Your
timeless memory
lives inside
shrieking endless pleas
to be relieved
relieved
of the prison
you consign it to.

Bent Box (Racist II)

Don't
get me wrong
I don't
love him
feel sorry for him.
I just see him,
see him,
see him.

My bent box
etches
his infant
memory
across
colour
time
and calculable thought
outside of math
he looks
quite human.

Bent Box (Christian)

Christians live in the middle of my bent box
crowding my woman relatives in its perfect corners
A circle of flesh drapes the sound
Christians make from under holy clothes
       "blessed be the meek
       for they shall inherit
       the earth . . ."
Before the icon in the house of God I query his son:
       Did you know what a long journey
       lay ahead for woman?

       The magnitude of your words
       the maleness of your intended
       meek
            silenced woman.

"I am the light"

       and forever your words
       paralysed the larynx
       of my half of humanity.

Our Father
       and forever birth was buried
       in the intricate.

Bent Box (Sensuality)

My body slid its litheness
from under a sky vaulted with thunder
pulled by the swollen storm of pain
expunged
empowered
feminine
        oneness.

I watched faces
ensconced in woman-flesh
blend into non-descript forms
while spirits
uniquely cultivated by time
sang
danced in sacred unison.

Robes whirl, blue pearled abalone buttons flashing
against red and black wool rectangles of dance.

The mystery of the world
feminine conception
rendered
immodest
by false
braggadocio.

Bent Box (Love)

Joyous blood
resides
not in my fingertips
       but
       in the thick
       pulsing manhood
       of cedar coloured man
anxious to bring me to that
sensuous
sacred place
only cedar
inspired to bent box
beauty
knows.

I relinquish nothing
by acknowledging my joy's source.
Power-outs have
no place
in the joy of the sacred.
Joy
knows not
coercive
force.

Bent Box (Sociology)

Who are these men
who disclaim
animal origins
pontificate from narrow
cavernous
perches
brag
in the name
of humanity?

      These men
who claim manhood
for all men
have never
peeked
inside the wall
of a bent box
where other
sensuous men
with womanly hearts
reside.

I imagine
hordes of corpulent
pink-skinned gentlemen
entrapped in boxes
of brutalized stone
ingesting
goblets of vineyard berries
aged

beyond useful nutrition
gabbling
nincomepoopetyjaw
about pleasure
pain
and white male
motivation.

All men . . .
and I remember
Hyak
in all his tumescent glory
seductively
persuading me
of the beauty
of my ways.

All men . . . How dare you
speak for *Hyak,*
cedar
raven
or any man
nurtured
in the intimate
knowledge
of earth's magnificent
endless
breast.

Bent Box (My Song)

My song hails
from a bent box
drums of earth tears
enjoys the unbending
of woman spirit
issued through a voice
cloaked
in androgynous souls.
This voice
penetrates silence
cracks barriers.

I can build
a bent box, shape its womanly contours
build fire from moss
light lives
sing man-song
birth children.
But I cannot penetrate
the dark hidden pleasures
of
my
womanhood.

Bent Box (Stone)

Old stone and bits of earth
signal the birthplace of seeds
nurtured by bent box
to re-people ancient hills.

Dawn splashes
yellow light
around her own contours
she gathers
slivers
of memory
seeds and light and swims
swims upriver
against whole tides
her hands cup tornado
and her memory sings tomorrow's
sweet
old
songs.

Bent Box (Youth)

songs mar silence . . . break seeds of memory . . .
fill bodies
with soft sounds
of different times.

Steady heart beat rhythms
heal tubercular desire in her mind
"want me" echoes impotent
below
the unrelenting hymn of drums.

Exhaustion
welcome slumber
dreams
rose
hillsides
recarve dream sleep.

Concrete borders
edge
the path
of her tornado
whole buildings spin
spin
helplessly
in the wake of dreams
virgin and unspoiled.

Outside her bent box
worlds sing
of cultural palaces
rich
with stupid drunkenness
fired water
unable to quiet sacred flames.

Video games
Seven Eleven
painted automobiles
shopping malls filled with useless baubles
call her
try me
take me
want me . . .
Desire
screams tense her body
"Listen"
whispers bent veins
Wood rings . . . windsong echoes . . .
tightens muscles
stilled by indecision.

Bent Box (Womanhood)

In my bent box sleeps my womanhood
the cedar red-brown hues of her walls
reflect
the colour of gramma's face.

My dead world lies between the lines
of her red earth grain
buried by silent hands,
hands too discouraged to appreciate
the colour of her womanly curves.

Bent Box (Raven)

Raven
conjure the image
of these others mind's
meanderings
I must
produce
three thousand words
about
the problems
of pleasure and pain
outside
the realm of poetry
story
and sacred knowledge.

Raven,
don't play with me.
I must walk the distance of this course.
"It's just another mountain to climb!"
I pack up my pemmican and *shtwehn*
and haul ass,
hurdle the non sense
of J. S.
the good old boy,
consume
words
until my eyes hurt.

Chee-chee-chee
I
understand.
focus on letter-words,
calculate
meanings:
given this, then that,
multiply pleasure
subtract pain
add apathy.
It's only a recipe
for cooking up humanity.

Choose base words
immoveable phrases
without hope
or urgency.
Batter them
into judiciary patterns.
Fire is not necessary
to prepare philosophy
just scrape multiples
of quantified notions
serve cold.
Profanity
after all
is best served raw.

I am
therefore I think.

Bent Box (Magic)

Magic
lives
in my bent box
bedroom.
Fire
satiated
by gentle
fingers
glides
along
well known
places
quiets
my
internal
tornado.

WARM WIND

Beware

I have felt wind-song
                caress my body
brought copper-coloured babies
                into earth's lush green
paddled the water of my ancestors.

I have stared wide-eyed at
                white men bulldozing
their way across my prairie green
awed by their big houses rising
                in their multitudes
to touch the sky.

I embraced Black mother's babies
                escaping slavery
slept alongside railroad coolies, bore
slant-eyed copper-gold and green-eyed
                wooly-haired young.

I once spoke the fat, sticky words
                that rattle the tongue
and reek of human suffering.
Words that battered my man
        abused my children
        salted the wounds of my sister,
denied that rain was sweet tears
                of woman-earth
paining to give birth.

Beware, settler,

> for the language of suffering
> humanity is breathing liberation
> to the winds of freedom.

Untitled

I have walked the length
       of human history,
honoured sun, moon, earth and sky,
basked in the fullness of life's bounty
gave children,
       my woman-gift to creation.

I have walked the length
       of human history,
laboured 'neath the settler's heat,
spoke the language Shakespeare spoke
learned of
       African slave and Chinese coolies.

I have walked the length
       of human history.
In my lands I embrace dark humanity,
'neath our common sky beats one drum-song,
liberation,
       nurture humanity's freedom,
our woman-gift to life.

My Box of Letters

(December 23, 1959)

I was only six when they forced me to take
the box of beastly letters.

We were not friends from the start
We resented each other.

They tripped over each other in crazy
senseless and ridiculous patterns.

They jumped around me defiantly
Higgledy-piggledy and round.

They got me in trouble, these mischievous
little rascals.

They hated me. They said it was because
I didn't understand them.

I jumped inside the box, grabbed them
and wrestled them down.

This didn't work, they fought hard.
There were twenty-six of them and I was only one.

(1991 afterthought on finding this, my first poem saved by my mother)

With diligence and persistence
I befriended them

I cajoled them, persuaded them for years
to make them behave.

Razzleberries

A thousand tiny thorns
   tear at my flesh
intense sun-heat blisters
   my black back.

Countless red berries
   bob and weave
     before me.

   Stinging nettles
morning mud, mosquitoes
     cow flies . . .

A heavy bucket pulls at my neck
arms upstretched, eyes squinting.

Still, I'd rather pick razzleberries
then vegetate before a typewriter.

Untitled

I could feel night
dark and cold
hear the hum of
the car
murmuring fear
cold steel
roaring fire

I felt the engine
cut out
heard footsteps
crunch gravel
felt hot breath
sear my
body

Hands clawing at
the flimsy cloth
protecting me
fists raining
against my face
hot rods tearing
at my flesh
my flesh
my birthing place

Mama

A warm drift of voices
overtop achin' feet
and freezing fingers

An absurd remark
a peal of rhythmic sound
listening to mama
laughin' at the crab shack.

twenty-nine years later
overtop an achin' back
and freezing fingers

an absurd remark
echoes rhythmic sound
my children are listening to mama
laughin' in the berry patch.

(Mama: I used to sit outside the crabshack listening to the sound of
you and the women working with you laughing and chatting to the
steady beat of pounding crabs. I laughed quietly to myself so you
wouldn't know I was there. I wanted to hear the stories, the laughter
and not be sent to play.

I didn't talk then. By the time I learned to speak the feelings and
thoughts I wanted to express were imprisoned. Imprisoned by the
reality of a hard existence. Voice and words found me alienated and
hungry to understand why.)

Light

light
dancing purple light
engages green
encircles
passes through one another
sways above grass blade tips
swings
on wind's wings
half lit
purple/grey shadows
enwrap the dancing throng
step lightly
oh so lightly
on stone's soft skin
dance, without beginning
without end
dance
murmurs peace
passion's dance
carefully
oh so carefully
colours amuse touch
vanish amid bright red smoke
stanchions of pine
on khaki hillsides
dotted with pale green sage
a glorious *soiree*
before summer's sleep

in autumn's cool
still
air.
bright light
retreats
into scents of pine and sage
kisses earth
—her breast heaves
          a contented sigh.

To My Children

Ask for nothing sweet child
for people will give what they can.
To ask is to imply the donor is selfish.
Take what is offered
to refuse is to offend,
insult the donor's gift as worthless.

Raise not your voice to your Elders,
do not argue with them.
State your opinion with modesty.

If rejected
understand you are but a child.
You do not understand your life
or the significance of experience.

Desire not what is best for you
but, what is best for others, therein
lies the secret of real happiness.

Be loyal to our unborn nation.
Strive to give your life to its future.

Columpa

Through wide set eyes,
the colour of burnt wood,
sparkling like sun
on a rain-soaked field
my dreamy-eyed child
watches the world.

An endless stream of dusky
smoke-skinned people
march in and out of her world.

      Big, giant people
             with commanding,
                    decisive ways
      warm hearts and gusty laughs.

Her eyes look beyond the people
that grow smaller as her world enlarges.

Thousands of details
make the dreamy lady's picture
details that etch themselves
firmly, in her mind.

Humour lights her life
like moon beams
ease the fear of dark.

Laughter from deep within her body;
shakes her, sending ripples of pleasure
to those around her . . .

Sunshine, moonbeams
dance around her.

Kiss mountaintops,
Caress the trees.

Never leave the heart
of my dreamy-eyed
moon-faced Columpa.

Northland

Northland . . . northland, my home,
a solitary child
perched atop a fallen log
breathing moss spirit
nurtured by wind-song.

Colour his fire-spirit
sun-gold, warm wind.
Paint his life with music,
fill his ears
with the spirit-breath
of his northland home.

Call me, my northland,
from the concrete sidewalks
and rain-drenched skid rows,
call the northland from within
that I may offer you
to the smouldering, leadened
children of the pavement.

Pavement child,
let the soft warm earth
of the northland
breathe fire into your cold body
that your spirit
might be kindled by the fire
of my northland
My northland, my home.

Ka-Nata

She sat on an unlit stove-top
the first three years of her life,
eyes wide open, mouth shut
and she watched people come in
and out of her life in endless streams.
She witnessed the undercurrents
the by-plays and the rivers of gossip
people paddle in.

The view from the stove
was full
round and all encompassing.

All of life begins
becomes and ends with story.
Academic theories
are but the leaky summations
of human stories.
She collected these stories
unencumbered by theory.
Stories
carefully crafted
from the layers of obstacles
hurdled and not hurdled
on their onward march to death.

Her self was a protected one. A self
totally at liberty to sit silently
watching the world
or caterwaul noisily among other children

busying their selves
with the work of playing at life.
There were no boxes
in which to stuff thoughts
ideas
relationships
neatly cut up
and wrapped to please the discerning eye.
No myriad of useless instructions
badgered
her consciousness into kinetic slavery.

No prohibitive laws
impeded her grasp
of the relation between self
and community—*Ka-Nata*
just the constant example
life presents to every self
to emulate
or disregard.

Choice was born in the self
on the stove, unlit, hard
unyielding. Choice, so inextricably
bound to community
love of difference
threaded its steely yarn
into the cloth of her.

The other world evidenced
her sense of choice
the soul of community.
Images of yak-yak-yakking

about self
and neighbourhoods
and the absence of choice
taught her about human
hypocrisy.

This other world
never done speaking of self
addresses spirit of community
destroys all vestiges of self
and *Ka-Nata*
in the name of this holy self.

She too rammed her choice
against the invisible fabric
of choicelessness
and experienced defeat.
She crashed
headlong into hidden barriers
constructed of apathy
conformity
and
communitylessness.

She plunged into the rivers
of the other world . . . red hot with zeal
and nearly drowned
in the undercurrent
of its influence.
From the embankment
she crawled to the top
of her ancestral mountains
to recover her self.

She watched
the multitudes below
exercise their sacred right of choice
in delusions of racial superiority
She watched while these delusions
rent great holes
in their own spirit
—no one was spared.

The web of autocratic discipline
white and cold
wound itself around the slim thread
of choice
choked and throttled
her sense of self.
She cried
in holy terror.

She struck blindly at the silken thread
shouting injustice to her gravediggers.
She howled
wept bitter tears
screamed until the sound
and the fury of it
buried the voice of *Ka-Nata*.

Shame exhausted the bodily dress
that housed her spirit . . . she collapsed
in a field of yellow flowers.
The wind gentled her body
the grass caressed her skin.
Sister sun rolled her healing light
across her tattered being.

In sleep
she dreamed of winged things
of vision total
and undespairing.
She dreamed of monarchs
in Brazilian meadows
lush green and unfree
monarchs flitting about
unable to light
sink roots
in their own soil.

Behind her stood
the truth of infinite grandmothers
ahead of her marched
the truth of infinite
progeny.
Legions
who cannot forsake *Ka-Nata.*

She understands panic at this
other world, monstrous in its magnitude
but she is not so otherly
as to believe the marriage of choice
and *Ka-Nata*—compelling in its
majesty—will not come.
The gentle bride of choice
cannot be forced to lie in the arms
of *Ka-Nata.*

Howling will not beckon her . . .
Multitudes must attend
the wedding party

whole nations are called forth.
Ka-Nata
the sleeping giant
will awaken without a howl.
The clatter and clang of machines
will be less deafening
the concrete less barren
Ka-Nata less impossible
and the earth will sing
a song of maternal hope.

But she understands, Mr. Ginsberg,
your need to HOWL

She could not have known this
had she not heard
your howl
from the rooftops
of a mountainless concrete desert.
She could not have thought this
had she not sat on a stove top
in another world.

Zeller's

Colours clutter boxes in Zeller's department store
bins of flaming red
      insulting lime
         green
    and
         bright pile
tier upon tier they suffocate
the slaves beneath

t-shirts	flash	immodest
in front	of racks	of burlesque
underwear	wild	and risque
unhidden	they stare	at the less
elegant	sale	shirts

In Solitude

In solitude
I uncoil
imagine
unravel memory
weave a perfect map
of solidarity
with blood
fire
ice and stone

In solitude
I imagine
souls stretched
across millenia
weeping
laughing
loving being
perfect being

beings
seeking communion
with the living
not the dead

In solitude
I envision
memories
of overdressed
over-fed lords
covered in trappings

of aliveness
drained of solitude
crowded with consumption
forming words
full of meaness
empty of compassion

In solitude
I see sharing
its heart cut out
profiteering
left naked
to pile inequities
bone upon bone
de-throating
birdsong

under the mantle
of a voice
shrieking
work, work, work

In dark dank
hovels
fair children
denied light
food
play-work
maddeningly
sweat blood
shed dry tears
and work

In solitude
I remember
rats, lice, filth
and disease
crawling inside bodies
of babies
accustomed to death
cutting lineage
out of their lives

Weariness
born in bodies
burdened by work

In cities
fetid with waste
children
stagger
to factories
sweat, stagger
to darken corners
for uncarnal knowledge
too old
for their dreams

Too battered to scream
life their horror
too innocent to resist
sleep their solitude
too bent to know
heaven their dream
their solitude denied
killing solidarity

and death their
only ecstasy
death their mate

In solitude
I imagine
bodies
mangled souls
denied access
to their sacred selves
insides weeping
outsides lashing
lashing
lashing

I imagine
hordes of breathing
survivors
their souls
a void
filled with hate
piled
tier upon tier
insides terrified
bodies
lurching

debased men
cast adrift from England
land in Newfoundland

I remember women
soft earth brown

dancing
swaying under virgin
skies
their flesh torn
scraped
mounted by men
seeking death
their only
ecstasy.

In memory
I imagine
solitude
solidarity
its death throes
earth weeping
tender
in her requiem
for dead love
sweet
in her silence
for lost love
hopeful
in her memory
of future

In madness
solitude
terrifies
enrages
fragments out lives
into angry
pieces

who need
to kill
kill
kill

madness
cannot recreate
remember
or nurture
cannot love
is not passionate
can only merge
with greater
madness

kill solidarity
kill humanity
kill oneness

In solitude
I climb mountains
empty my self
of dispassion
imagine
memory
perfect
in its isolation

In perfect
isolation
my memory
sings sweet songs
of love

to others
in our loneness
I imagine
love
humankindness
passion

In imaging memory
stone speaks
clings to earth
fire water and we

Stone song
murmurs
of newfound love
sing stone . . .
unravel
the self
sing stone . . .
great spirit
demands
great union
sing
stone . . .

In solitude
Murdoch sits
my stone and his in hand
remembering
solidarity
trying not to forget
rebirthing
being

perfect being
across
this long distance
of time.

Ta'ah

I wanted to escape your smiling eyes,
go beyond their warm black
I wanted to wrap my spirit around
other feelings

Flee to unknown places
travel across time
to a different world
I didn't want to be you

You were still
I ran
You walked steadily
I refused

You were poetic
modest
in your presentation
of language

I, vulgar
brassy
repelling the soft murmur
of your voice

Manipulated
you called upon grandmothers
"let me be useful
one more moment"

Let me give one more second
of blissful reprieve, sock
life's crystal shards
safely in our lineage

I didn't want to be you,
but the embers
of truth behind your eyes
kindled my passion

I travelled
to places
to relieve others
and tormented myself

I drank clear visions
from the lives of saints
whose demons made them blind,
watched my own fire catch

I went willingly, Ta'ah
to places where flames
licked gardens of eden
melted my insides

Bled lava rock
across emerald hillsides
exploded storms
of insidious words

poured black ash
across green growth
listened carefully
to tree lamenting death

in the ashes of cedars
burial
our Grandmothers breathed
stories of unparalysed growth

I saw movement
purple, green and gold
spirits dancing,
loving,

exalting earth
in all its tormented
beauty
"crystal," Ta'ah, "is not clear"

you saw coal burn red hot
dusty black
to fired diamond
a jagged-edged miracle

"Just birth," you smiled,
"creation, re-creation,
new paths cut
from old patterns"

Letter to Jamilla!
(Who sneaked off to Hong Kong)

Bring me back bamboo,
unsplintered by Europe's touch.

Bring me back the scent of Hong Kong
unhindered by decadent rot.

Unhindered:

(T'is a gentle word
light to the touch
rhythmic,
sweet and small,
deep in meaning
colourful,
musical,
but lost to me.)

Unhindered
will have to do.

Natural Rhythm

(After reading *Degrees of Green* by Jeannette Armstrong)

Winter days fall under cold winds
whirling about skeletal trees
bent beneath drapes of white
struggling for light
from a place of dark solitude
to create new shapes—portents of dawn
driven upward from earth's centre
to surface at the tip of ice crystals
cracking from the burden of pulchritude.

Sound Poem

(For Willie Armstrong)

This is my last dance across old horse trails
My last prance between cactus and dust-dressed sage
Horse under-me listens to my tongue's soft murmurs
this language stretched thin inside fading chords
picks its way along old notes of fine sound
We agree on this *Okanagan-kinda-talk*   him and I

Dedicated to the Anishnawbekwe

(who founded the Barrie Native Friendship Centre)

Words are breath tracks speaking to those who have already left their
            imprint
on our lives.

These words whisper softly from just behind the footprints of those
            who
first imagined this house.

Because so many of those who imagined this house were women it
            quickly became
a reality.

I look upon the journey you must have taken from the moment of
            conception to
this moment when our breath tracks speak to honour you.

I picture the endless nights of huddling over coffee, dreaming up the
            next step,
knocking down obstacle after obstacle.

I listen to the memories of phone calls to friends, to neighbours, to
            officials, even to
foes, to make this building happen.

I watch from behind you as your murmurs join each others words,
            listen to the words link

themselves to others until, the words became a mortgage, a building, a
program . . .

I see the moments when, nearly disheartened, overworked and not
quite there yet,
some of you must have considered throwing in the towel.

The sighs around the table must have occasionally been heavy, then
some one of you
told a joke and the spirit changed.

I know before the programs, before the building, before the mortgage,
there was an
amazing clutch of women, who journeyed to our success.

Amazing women with sure feet, endless energy and a great vision of
community, *Migwech* to
each and every one of you.